THE YOUNG PIAI

FIRST BOOK

by DENES AGAY

Contents

- The KEYBOARD of the piano has *white keys* and *black keys*.

- The black keys are arranged in groups of *two's* and *three's*.

- The white keys are in a row. They are named after the first seven letters of the alphabet:
A B C D E F G

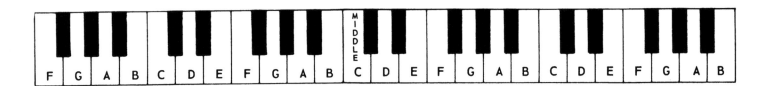

- Music is written on a system of five lines called the STAFF.

- Piano music is written on two staffs:

This staff, headed by the TREBLE CLEF, is for higher notes, usually played by the *right hand*.

This staff, headed by the BASS CLEF is for lower notes, usually played by the *left hand*.

The two staffs joined by a brace are called the GRAND STAFF.

- For easier reading the staff is divided by BAR LINES into MEASURES.

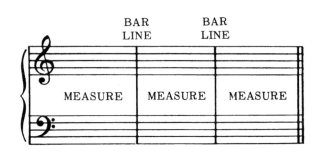

● Within a piece of music each measure usually has the same number of counts, as indicated by a TIME SIGNATURE, two numbers at the head of the staff.

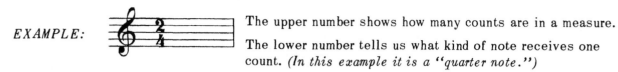

EXAMPLE:

The upper number shows how many counts are in a measure.

The lower number tells us what kind of note receives one count. *(In this example it is a "quarter note.")*

● There are different kinds of notes, depending upon how long they are held:

QUARTER NOTE ♩ is held for *one* count.

HALF NOTE ♩ is held for *two* counts.

DOTTED HALF NOTE ♩. is held for *three* counts.

WHOLE NOTE 𝅝 is held for *four* counts.

● For playing the piano our fingers are numbered. *The thumb is the first finger* on each hand.

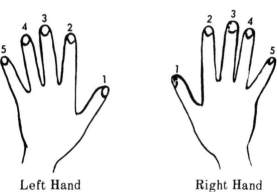

Left Hand   Right Hand

NOTE CHART
THE NOTES OCCURRING IN THIS BOOK; THEIR LETTER-NAMES AND
THEIR LOCATION ON THE KEYBOARD

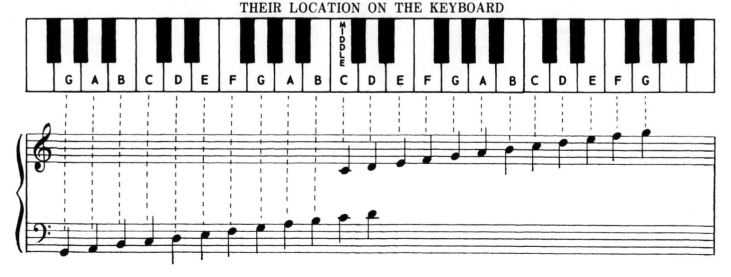

MARCH FOR THE RIGHT HAND

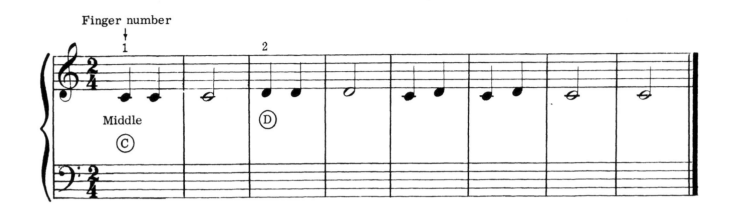

MARCH FOR THE LEFT HAND

"RIGHT AND LEFT" MARCH

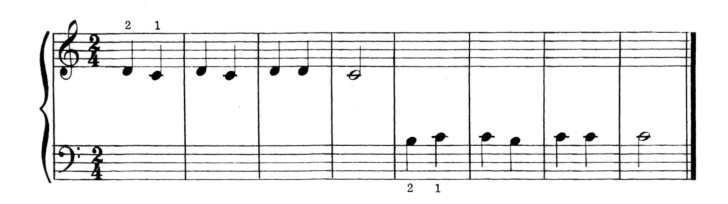

In every piece, new notes, when they occur the first time, are marked by their letter names. Using the NOTE CHART on page 3, mark each new note with an **X**.

HUMMING TWINS

SKIPPING ALONG

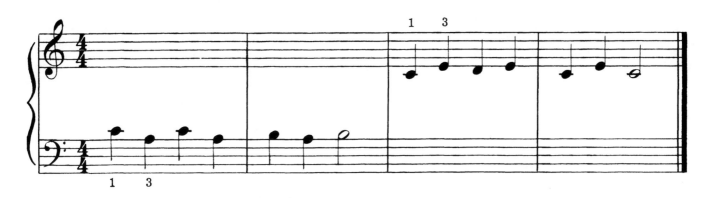

Now try "SKIPPING ALONG" this way: play the left hand starting on the C eight notes (keys) lower and the right hand starting on the C eight notes higher. (On the keyboard the distance of eight notes is called an <u>Octave</u>.)

DA0001

MORNING SONG

f (forte) = loud
p (piano) = soft

EVENING SONG

EVENING SONG WITH BELL

Play the right hand an Octave higher.

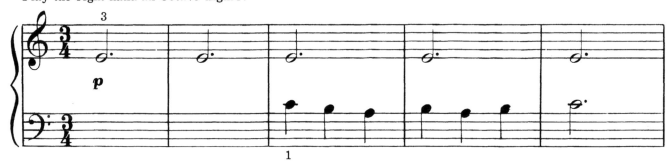

MUSICAL PROVERB

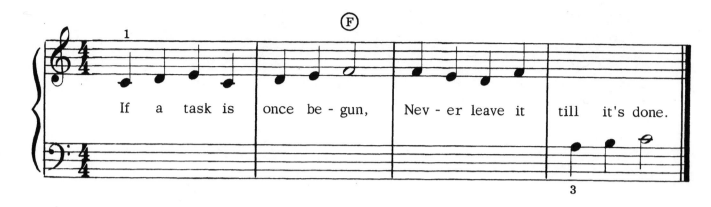

If a task is once be - gun, Nev - er leave it till it's done.

ON THE SWING

8

<u>CHORALE</u> is another word for a church hymn.

CHORALE

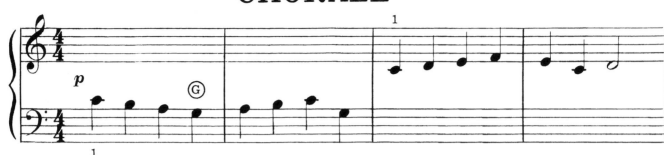

YANKEE DOODLE

Traditional

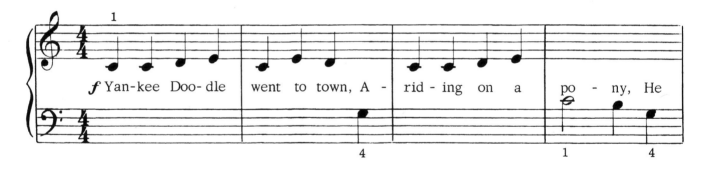

f Yan-kee Doo-dle went to town, A - rid - ing on a po - ny, He

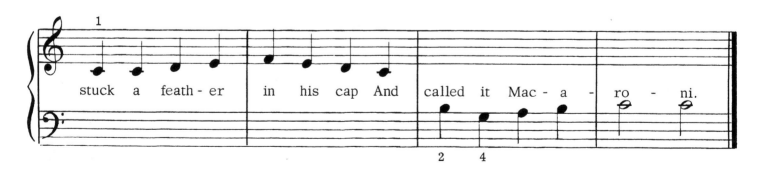

stuck a feath - er in his cap And called it Mac - a - ro - ni.

Optional duet part
for Yankee Doodle

THE YODELER

DOWN IN THE VALLEY

Folk Song

The curved line connecting one note with the very next note on the same line or space is called a TIE.
It means that the second note is not played but held for its full time value.

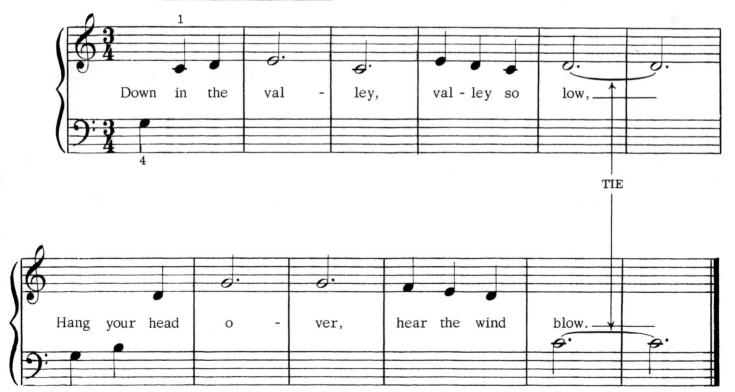

Down in the val - ley, val - ley so low,_____

Hang your head o - ver, hear the wind blow._____

TIE

10

A curved line *(slur)* connecting several different notes means that these notes belong to one melodic unit called a PHRASE: it also means that these notes should be played in a smoothly connected manner, LEGATO.

QUESTION AND ANSWER

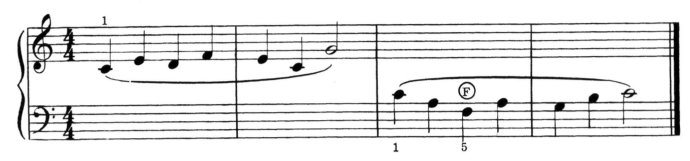

Repeat "Question and Answer" by playing the right hand an Octave higher and the left hand an Octave lower.

WALTZING ON THE SIDEWALK

The Quarter rest (𝄽) has the same time value as the Quarter note.

(𝄽 = ♩ = one count).

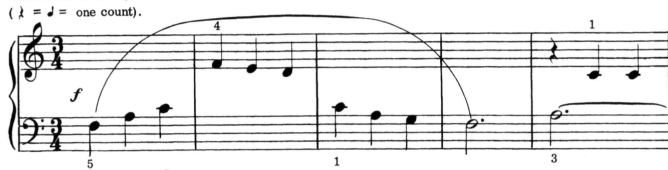

The small dot at the note head is the sign of STACCATO: you play the note short and detached.

PLINK-PLUNK

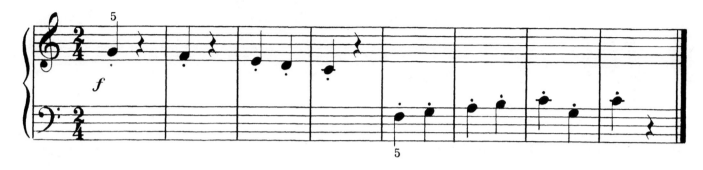

Repeat "Plink-Plunk"; this time play the right hand an Octave higher and the left hand an Octave lower.

THE SAD CLOWN

TEMPO MARK - Tempo is the speed, or rate of movement in music. *mf (mezzo forte)* = medium loud.

Moderately

The SHARP sign (♯) placed in front of a note means that this note is <u>raised</u> to the nearest higher note: you play the very next key to the right, black or white.

THE HAPPY CLOWN

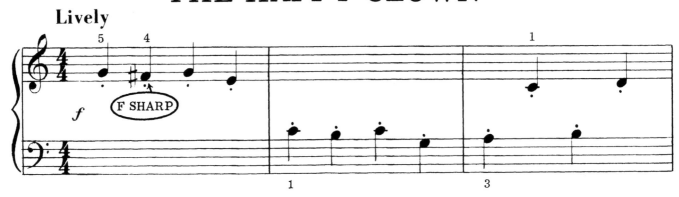

♫ These are two Eighth notes; they equal the time value of one Quarter note. Two Eighth notes receive one count. (♫ ♩ = ♩ = one count.)

PARADE OF TEN LITTLE INDIANS

Traditonal

Walking tempo

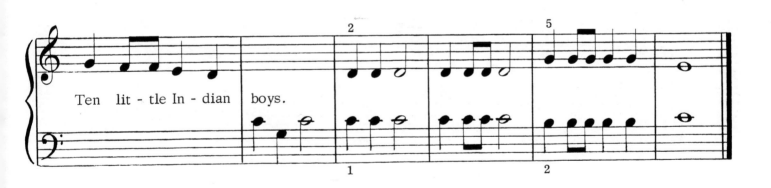

Optional duet part

The WHOLE REST 𝄻 indicates silence in one whole measure whether it has four, three or two counts.

CLOUDY DAY

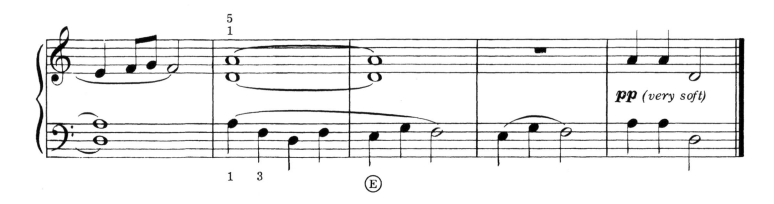

SHEPHERD DANCE

THE BRASS BAND

> = accent mark

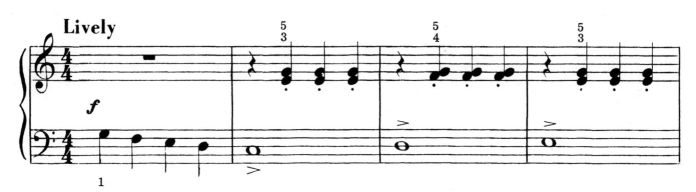

REPEAT SIGN

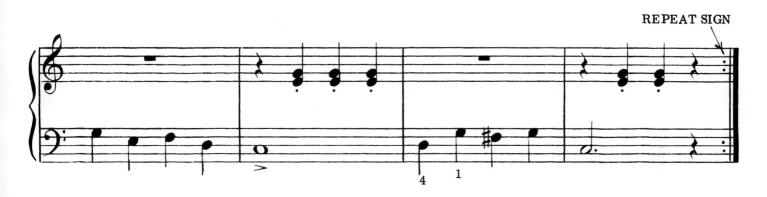

LOVE SOMEBODY

Folk Song

mp (mezzo piano) = medium soft

Play "Love Somebody" again with the right hand an Octave higher.

DA0001

The FLAT sign (♭) placed in front of a note means that this note is lowered: you play the very next key to the left, black or white.

THE MANDOLIN PLAYER

Moderately

THE FIRST BLUES

This piece begins with the last beat of a measure. Notice that this starting note completes the last measure where the fourth beat is missing.

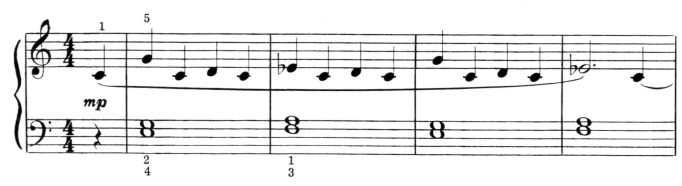

Play "The First Blues" again with the right hand an Octave higher.

BARCAROLLE is a piece of music in the style of the songs of the Venitian gondoliers.

BARCAROLLE

Gently floating

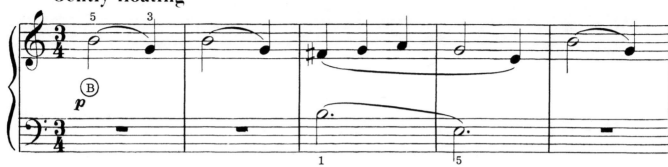

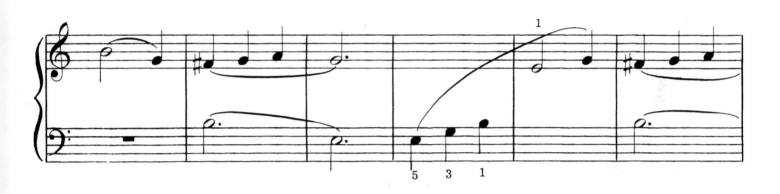

DO YOU KNOW THE MEANING OF THESE WORDS AND SIGNS ?	
1. An OCTAVE	5. The TIE
2. LEGATO	6. The SHARP sign (♯)
3. *f* and *p*	7. 𝄾
4. STACCATO	8. The FLAT sign (♭)

18

The HALF REST ━ has the same time value as the Half note. (━ = 𝅗𝅥 = two counts).

THE ACROBAT

Briskly

Cross the left hand
over the right hand.

The flats placed at the head of
the staffs mean that every B in
the piece is lowered to B flat.

HOE DOWN

Lively

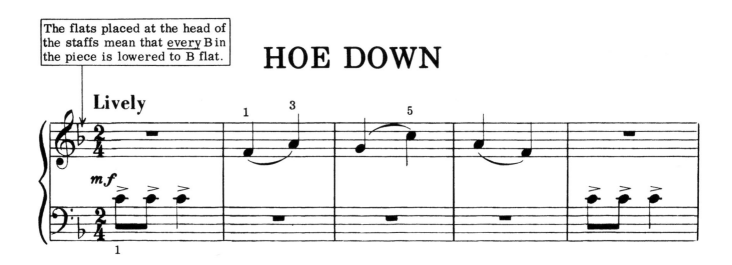

THE MERRY-GO-ROUND

Moderately

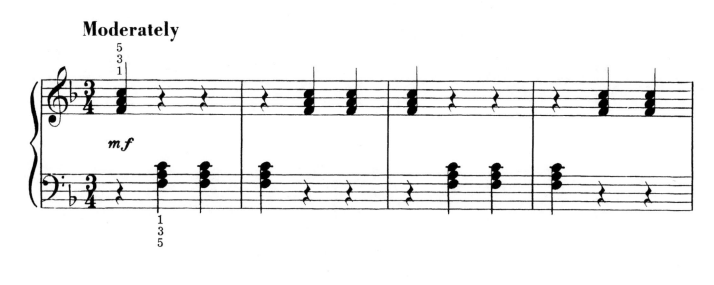

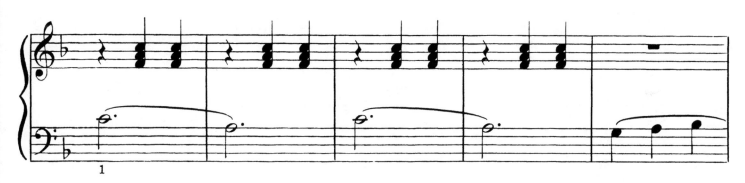

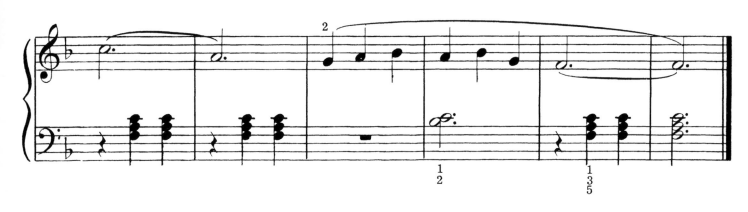

A line at the note head ($\bar{\rho}$) means that you give the note a little extra weight and hold the key down for the note's full time value. This is called TENUTO.

COUNTRY FIDDLER

THE HAUNTED CLOCK

CIRCUS POLKA

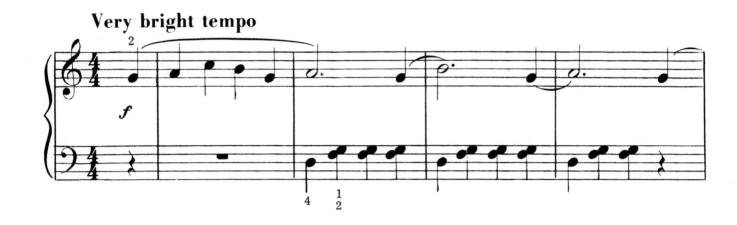

DANCE OF THE COSSACKS

Ukrainian Folk Tune

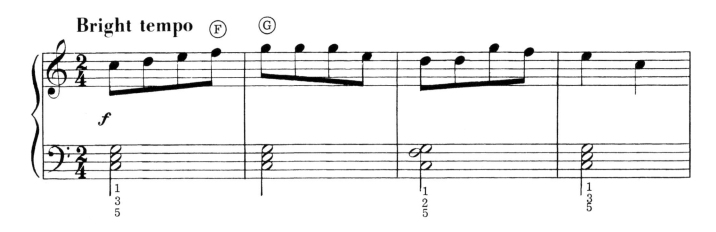

The sign of NATURAL (♮) cancels a sharp or a flat.   Placed in front of a note it means that the note is no longer raised or lowered.

LITTLE PRELUDE

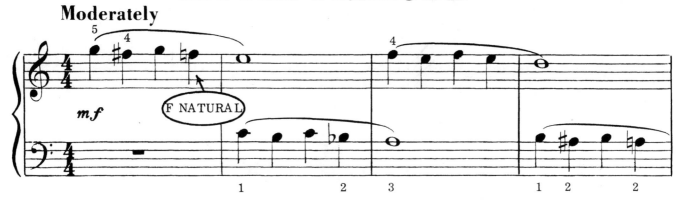

NIGHT MUSIC

Every F in this piece is raised to F sharp.

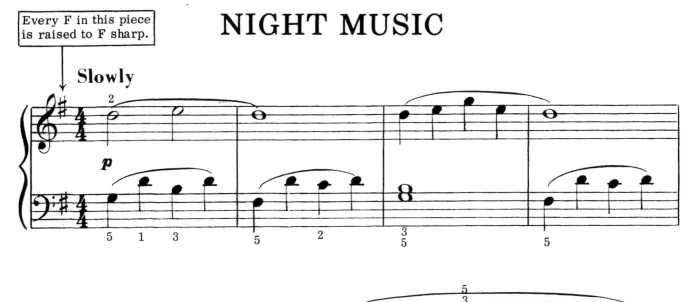

THE CHASE

CRESCENDO = gradually louder
RIT. (RITARDANDO) = gradually slower

Lively

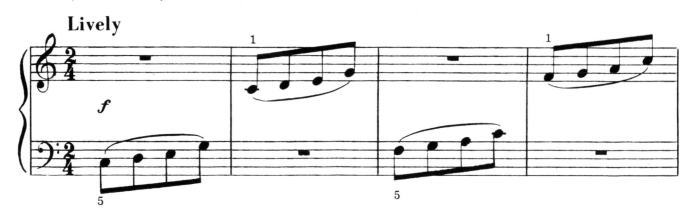

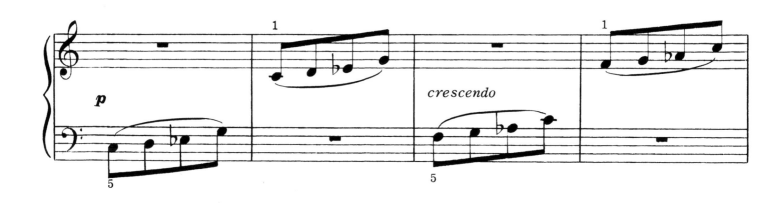

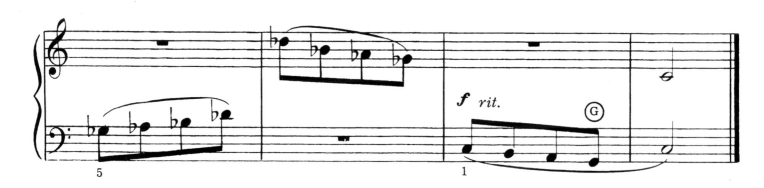